This book belongs to

_____

Dad and I
Let our Farts Fly!

By
Humor Heals Us

It's Father's Day, which makes me so happy,
And here's the reason why.
We celebrate my amazing Dad
As Dad and I let our farts fly!

I set the alarm to wake up early
To give Dad a surprise.
When I get out of bed with a morning toot,
It brings tears to my eyes!

We go on a family ride to the park.
I sit up nice and tall.
My helmet saves me from mighty toots
Because if I smelled that, I would fall!

Dad rides so fast along the road,
My tummy gets all jiggly.
And when we hit a bump I pop off
Which makes us both so giggly!

Laying out the picnic rug
Should be done with ease.
But not when Dad and I let one rip,
The rug flies away in the breeze!

We eat lemon tarts which are tasty.
I have six in one hour.
But now I'm doing lemon farts
Which smell incredibly sour!

We play a game to see who can keep
The frisbee in the air.
Dad and I have a fart filled advantage,
That really isn't fair.

My sister tries to join in on the game
She thinks that it looks fun.
But she gets in the way of one of Dad's farts,
And it knocks her on her bum!

Some ants try to steal our leftover food,
While we're off having a play.
But they don't realize that our farts,
Just will not go away!

We lie on our tummies,
With our bums facing up, we fart into the sky.
Which means we alter the flight path,
Of three planes flying by!

Then, we pack up and head on home,
Dad's speed is up to 53.
And now it's not just our farts that fly,
Right now so are weeeeeeee!

I'm exhausted when we get back home
After all that stinky play.
But being with my family made it
The best ever Farter's Day!

That night, as Dad tucks me into bed,
Even though the room smells bad,
He gives me a kiss goodnight and I say,
'I really love you, Dad!'

www.ingramcontent.com/pod-product-compliance
Lightning Source LLC
Chambersburg PA
CBHW042024090426
42811CB00016B/1728